CONTENTS

3

4

No other door, no other Way

No other door, no other way
Will lead you to Jesus
Except the truth.
No other door, no other way
Will lead you to peace
Except the cross of Jesus.
No other cross, no other door
Will save you from hell
Except the way of Jesus.
His way is the right way,
Always the Saviour,
Never the sinner.
No other Lord will protect you
As much as my Lord Jesus,
For he will hold you
In his everlasting arms
To protect you from Satan,
To protect you from Hell.

The foolish man built his house upon the sand

The foolish man built his house upon the sand
And the rain came falling down;
The floods arose,
The winds they came,
The foolish man built his house upon the sand
And the house fell flat.

Jesus looked upon him in awe
wondering why he was so foolish,
This man who never followed God's way
But went in the world in his own,
The foolish man who built his house upon the sand
While the rain came tumbling down.

He never asked for help,
He never asked for Jesus,
This foolish man who built his house upon the sand.
The floods they rose,
The winds they came,
And the house fell flat.

Jesus, give me a heart which is pure within

Jesus, give me a heart which is pure within,
A heart full of kindness, strength, and warmth;
A heart which will render,
A heart which will grow
A love that never ends,
A love which always grows.
Jesus, give me a heart which is pure within,
Understanding, guidance and solitude,
A quietness which comes closer to you.
Jesus, give me a heart which is pure within,
A Lord who will lead me
To pastures new,
Deep down feelings of you, Lord Jesus,
A love so deep, so passionate
It never ends,
But keeps on growing inside me
Until the day I die.

Graces

Father, at this feast
We lay our eyes upon one another
To see what we are eating.
For the lumps in our pudding
And the soggy bread,
For the fizz and not the beer,
For the sausage, not the lamb
I thank you, Lord,
For providing this.

We ask your blessing on this meal
For the pudding that is lumpy
And the dough that just provides
For the throwing of the sausages,
And the fights around the table.
We ask your blessing on this, our meal,
And look forward to the next time
When we can start again.

For food and all that provide it,
For the catering at the vicarage
And the wife that cannot cook,
For a vicar who never arrives,
For he knows who prepares this, our grub,
And praise the Lord, it is not he,
But the vicar's wife that prepares our meals
And Lord, make her cook,
For we're sick of stodge
And fry ups.

To God who gives our daily bread,
The loaves of fishes
And the sheaf,
For the wheat in the fields
And the spread on our plates,
For providing this, our meal,
I thank you, Lord, for this.

Who Do You Say I Am?

'Who do you say I am'? said he
Raising his eyes up above;
His friends knew, without doubt
That he was a friend of love.

'Who do you say I am?' said he,
Using the gifts of Jesus
To love thousands, and everyone knew
He was the creator of joy.

'Who do you say I am?' said he,
Bidding a tidal wave be still;
In the great calm they all knew
That he was indeed peace.

'Who do you say I am?' said he
Gently holding a child;
He was great, our patience revealing
He was so meek and mild.

'Who do you say I am?' said he,
As the pathway of gladness he trod;
And we replied, 'Thou art our Lord,
The Son of the living God.'

Come, dearest Jesus

Come, dearest Jesus, descend and dwell
By gracious love live inside us all
Then we shall know the power of your love
The joy inside our hearts.

Come, fill our lives with heavenly love
Make our world a better place
And teach us to serve you
So that we may live in peace.

Now to the Lord whose power is great ,
We sing our praises for evermore
Be everlasting in our hearts
Bring with you a joyous heart.

(Chorus)
He lives!
He lives!
Hallelujah!
For he is King
Over all the earth.

Let us with a gladdened mind

Let us with a gladdened mind
Rejoice, the Lord is King;
He came to save us
To take away our sin;
For his mercies will endure
Ever faithful, ever sure.

Let us with a gladdened mind
Be filled with love anew
By him our Lord up above,
Who came to rule the earth;
For he came to save us,
To gladden each and every heart;
Let us with a gladdened mind
Rejoice, the Lord is king.

Let us with a gladdened mind
Praise the Lord, for he is kind;
He shows us the way,
Leads us from the grave
Into his holy place,
Where there is peace
And a bed.

Oh Come, Oh Come, Lord Jesus

Oh Come, Oh come, Lord Jesus,
Enrich our frozen hearts;
Teach us to love you,
To adore you and worship you
In your everlasting love.

Oh come, Oh come, Lord Jesus,
Take captive Israel;
We mourn a lonely life without your love,
To taste your caress,
To tend your feet.

Oh come, Oh come, Lord Jesus,
Mend our broken hearts;
Oh come, Lord, to take away our sin.
Yours is the glory
For ever and ever.

I Know inside my redeemer lives

I know inside my redeemer lives
My heart sings out his songs ;
By his love and everlasting love
He shines inside my heart.

May the Word of God grow inside
Into this cold and heartless heart;
Fill us up with love anew
And redeem us from Satan.

Lord, that I may learn from you
To walk your path of righteousness ;
Come, Father, teach us how to pray
And live inside your heart.

Of my boasted wisdom spoiled,
Young and helpless as a child,
Bring with you the truth of righteousness
So that I may walk in your light.

Hear me, O Shepherd of Israel

Hear me, O Shepherd of Israel,
You that lead your flock to pasture;
You that are enthroned upon high
Before Man, I beseech you
Your kingdom come for evermore.

Hear me, O Shepherd of Israel,
You have fed us with your love,
You endow us with your wisdom,
You have cried tears over us
Through your undying love.

Hear me, O Shepherd of Israel,
Restore in us the faith of God,
Enrich our souls with your peace
Like the doves that fly up high
Gracious as your love.

You cleared the ground before us,
You enriched our souls,
You raised our hearts,
So that there is peace
And harmony
For evermore.

From the Lord of the World

From the Lord of the World
Comes a joyous heart
For he brings with him warmth, comfort
And good things
That only he can bring.
He delivers all of us from evil,
He will rest our weary bones,
He will be there in our bad times
And even in our sadness
When we are just run down.
In our happy days
He is there to guide us
The Lord is our protector from the bad,
He washes away our sins.
From the Lord of the World
Comes plenitude, many offerings
That he showers all around us.
He loves a cheerful giver
Who helps mankind in many ways.
He releases us from the devil
And condemns the Satan curse.
The Lord of the World is Jesus
And I pledge my troth to him
For he will always protect me
In the good times
And the bad.

How lovely is your dwelling place

How lovely is your dwelling place,
The peace that surrounds us,
The love that overflows within you,
That does enrich our hearts.

Come, O saviour, and behold us,
Live within us for evermore.
(Chorus)
Raise up our arms,
Lift up our spirits,
Be within forevermore.

How lovely is your dwelling place,
Blessed are those that praise you
For your love is so great,
Your heart so pure,
Indeed you are true
Until the end.

Come, O Saviour, and behold us,
Live within us for evermore.
(Chorus)
Raise up our arms,
Lift up our spirits,
Be within for evermore.

Jesus is my guide

Jesus is my guide,
My Saviour,
My all.
He rescues me from the crowd
And carries me up high;
For I am a believer
Of the man named Christ;
For he lives in me.
Like you and me
He guides me through the pain and hurt,
He keeps me safe from harm,
He wraps his arms around
And takes away the tears.
Jesus is my guide,
My soulmate,
My ideal.
For he is perfect
In every form;
Creating the Earth,
The Planets,
The World.
He will always be there for you and me
Until the day we die;
Then he'll carry each believer
Into his Kingdom Come.

Prayer

Some tell us that prayer is in the mind
But for me, it is in the heart.
That prayer is the only result
Is he only comfort we find,
That God does not answer – but answer he does.
I have knelt down in his church
And I have received.
My faith has grown stronger,
And my love deeper.
I have seen God reach down from heaven above
Reach out his arms
In a quiet solitude.
He has moved mountains, touched each and every person,
We know God – he works miracles
He works in a wonderful way,
So reach out and touch him,
He is just waiting for you
To touch him.

I believe in Jesus

I believe in Jesus
Who created heaven and earth,
Source of light and wisdom
bringing wisdom and power to earth.

I believe in God the Saviour
The father of mankind,
Who was crucified for us
To wash away our sins.

I believe in the holy spirit
guide in heaven and earth,
A pledge that we inherit
To live our lives on earth.

Then honour, glory and respect
The great Lord's name on high,
He that washes away the sin
And forgives our foolish ways.

Come, dearest Jesus

Come, dearest Jesus, descend and dwell
By gracious love live inside us all
Then we shall know the power of your love
The joy inside our hearts.

Come, fill our lives with heavenly love
Make our world a better place
And teach us to serve you
So that we may live in peace.

Now to the Lord who's power is great
We sing our praises for evermore
Be everlasting in our hearts
Bring with you a joyous heart.

(Chorus)
He lives
He lives
Hallelujah
For he is king
Over all the earth.

From heaven you came

From heaven you came
Oh glorious Lord,
To take away our sin
Wash clean our souls.
To uplift us in your glory
To hold us up high,
To love the people on earth
To revel your glory.

There in his garden of Eden
Our heavy load he chose to bear,
His heart was heavy with sorrow
As he listened to our prayers.
His hands bore the scars of nails
We worshipped at his feet,
'Forgive us Lord, we have sinned'
Take away our pain.

A crown with many crowns

A crown with many crowns
Wears our Lord Jesus
Hark, how the angels sing
To our risen Lord
Of him who died for us
To cast away our sins
A great god and king
A crown with many crowns

Crown him the Lord of life
A man so holy and eternal
Crown him the king of creation
And lives that death may die
For he died for us
Rose for us
To be our eternal king
A crown with many crowns
is our great god and king

Blessed is the Lord

Blessed is the Lord
For he reigns on high
He reigns on high
He reigns on high
Blessed is the Lord
He reigns on high
He reigns on high

He is my saviour
Praise be the Lord
Praise be the Lord
Praise be the Lord
He is my saviour
Praise be the Lord
Praise be the Lord

The Lord is my strength
And my salvation
And my salvation
And my salvation
The Lord is my strength
And my salvation
And my salvation

Blessed is the Lord
For he reigns on high
He reigns on high
He reigns on high
Blessed is the Lord
He reigns on high
He reigns on high

God's Greatest Word

It was like a breath of fresh air
God's greatest word
For he gave to us his only son
Jesus
Born of Mary
He died for our sins
He gave us life
Jesus
Who loves everybody
A light in the darkness
Our heavenly being
Declare
God's greatest word
Let the words of the almighty
Overwhelm my soul
My life
My all

All the glorious names

Of all the glorious names
Jesus is above all
For he gave us prayer
He gave us a heart
To gladden each and every one

Of all the glorious names
Jesus is the name
Holy Jesus, Lord is seeking
To enlighten us
In his name is the power
And the glory
His heart is pure
When in heaven soaring
To salute a glorious name

Of all the glorious names
Jesus is above all
For he gave us prayer
He gave us a heart
To gladden each and every one

Joy to the World

Joy to the World
Jesus has risen
A halo of bright light shines
In the almighty heaven
Jesus the name above all
In the Lord's heaven
Come to us
And sing with us
Your praises as we pray

(Chorus)
Joy to the world
And to every nation
Lift up your hearts
So as he can hear
Your happy songs
Up in heaven

Joy to the world
And in love adoring
Who with perfect wisdom
Came to live with us all
God who sent his son
So that we can live
A happy life
A fulfilled one
One day up in heaven

Rejoice Rejoice

Rejoice, Rejoice
The Lord is king
For he shall reign
Over all the Earth

His kingdom is as one with God
He is eternal bliss and kingdom come
For his heart is pure as gold
And his love goes on for evermore

Rejoice, Rejoice
The Lord is king
For he shall reign
Over all the Earth

His love goes on for evermore
The cross that bore him
Now stands alone
For he has risen above to heaven
To be at his father's right hand

Rejoice, Rejoice
The Lord is king
For he shall reign
Over all the Earth

How firm his foundation

How firm his foundation
The glory of the lord
As strong as an ox
As great as his refuge
He holds us
And he tends us
To shape and caress us
As our lives go on

How firm his foundation
When in heaven we arise
To sit at his right hand
And listen to his stories
To say the great hallelujah
To our lord and king
To rise from the ashes
And to be as one with him

Eternal depth

Eternal depth of love divine
Shield us from our sins
Hold us in your loving arms
Enrich us with your love

To mould us and caress
Each and every one
For love is eternal
And life is bliss
How bright your light
Over all the Earth

To who we cloak your
Our flesh, soul, Spirit
Comes to you
Our lord in heaven
Protect us
As we come to love you
Each and every day

Eternal depth of love divine
How wide your healing power
To your fiery love for us
And our hearts forevermore

Preserve Me, O God.

Preserve me, O God,
For in you I have taken refuge
To anoint me
To caress me
To uplift me
In your arms.

Preserve me, O God,
Feed me with your love
For I have sinned
Against all odds
Anoint me with your love.

I have said to the Lord,
'All my good depends on you'
As ate those in who I can trust
Anoint me with your love

Preserve me, O God,
I will bless the Lord;
Therefore my heart is glad
My spirit rejoices
That I am at one with God.

I will sing

I will sing the praises
Of my wonderful King,
How he left the earth
To rise up to his Lord ;
He came back to save us
He died for our sins;
Yes, I'll sing the wondrous songs
That indeed make him King

I was lost, but he found me
Forlorn and bitter
And cold right through;
But his heart gave me gladness
His arms held me close
Days of darkness are now long gone,
As Jesus lives
I will sing.

Dear Father

Dear Father, your love is wonderful
Your heart is kind and pure
Your hands are gentle, your face is kind
I reach out and touch you
To feel your voice.
You draw me in with a loving kindness
You lift me up to a great height
However deep that I may sink;
You pull me back to your great side
However far that I may wander;
You follow me
And lead me back
To your chosen path,
The path of mankind,
And even when I plunge into greater depths
You raise me up again.
Dear Father,
Thank you for being just you
For sheltering me
And all your sheep
And so I will rest in your presence
With an everlasting love
And a greater kindness
That only you can show.

You are a little man

You are a little man
And a very little man are you.
You climbed into a sycamore tree
For the Lord you wanted to see
And when the Lord went past,
On his little donkey,
He looked into your tree
And said, "Now, little man, come down
For I'm coming to your house.
I'm coming for my tea".

Then you were so big
So proud that the Lord spoke to you
For as you climbed down
your heart missed a beat.
Your footsteps ran ahead of you
As you felt your knees give way
For the Lord you wanted to see
And see him, you sure did.

Justified by faith

Justified by faith we have in the Lord
We have peace with God
Our Saviour of mankind
Peace with God
Everlasting Jesus
Who died for us on the cross
To save us from sin
To save us from ourselves
To keep us safe from the storm
Through our lord Jesus Christ

Keep me true to yourself
Everlasting Lord of mankind
Justified by Christ, we have a light
The light of hope, for each of us
For Jesus knows our weaknesses
He knows our strengths
He knows our ways
He knows our hopes
He has a light
For each and every one of us.

Lord of Glory

Lord of Glory, Lord of Light
Lord of creation and majesty
Lord of strength and might
Amid the clouds and the sun
Though unworthy as we are
He tends to us, each one
Now to worship and to uphold
Now for resurrection and beyond
As in Christ, we praise
Praise the everlasting Lord.

Love the world though his eyes
Love the world through praise
For in God we have one family
Universal in it's way
Lord of Glory, Lord of Light
Lord of creation and majesty
For you are our one true Lord
Our holy friend
In the heaven's up above
Laying out our resting place
For our weary bones.

Which of you?

Which of you shall have a friend
A friend like my Lord Jesus
For with Jesus you're not troubled in the mind
You feel exalted and uplifted
You would ask for his never ending guidance
If you were in need

Which of you shall have a friend
If his knocks were often heard
He would raise you to the skies
Uphold you and adore you
For you're unique in his eyes
Each and every one of us

Ask, Seek, and you will find
You will find my friend Jesus
God the Father knows your need
And to anyone that knocks
A door will open
Into the light of heaven
Taking you into a new day.

I belong to Jesus

I belong to Jesus,
Therefore I can sing,
I can sing his praises,
I can surrender my heart,
I can touch his hand
For I'm safe and happy
Underneath the stars.

I belong to Jesus,
I help to do good to all,
I have a cheerful heart
I can touch his heart,
I can meet his needs.
When the days take me
Into his everlasting love,
Dear father, help me to be kind
To mend each broken heart,
To heal every broken bone
That lies shattered on the ground,
To heal the lies
And amend the truth
That will take me to holy ground.

From heaven you came

From heaven you came
Oh glorious Lord,
To take away our sin
Wash clean our souls.
To uplift us in your glory
To hold us up high,
To love the people on earth
To revel your glory.

There in his garden of Eden
Our heavy load he chose to bear,
His heart was heavy with sorrow
As he listened to our prayers.
His hands bore the scars of nails
We worshipped at his feet,
'Forgive us Lord, we have sinned'
Take away our pain

We give God thanks

We give God thanks,
for all we do
for all we see
from this day on .
to worship him
and to adore him,
We give God thanks
for all we do.

We give God thanks
for the birds and bees,
for uplifting us to Him on high
for taking away our sins.

We give God thanks
for all our skills,
Jesus hands how they reach out
for those who suffer long,
to help the anxious and the ill
We give God thanks.

Praise Jesus, the King of Glory

Praise, Jesus, the king of glory
to his feet my troubles come
Pain and suffering
healing ,glory
To the Lord my praise I sing

Alleluia, Alleluia
To the Lord my praise I sing

Praise Jesus for his grace and love
to our children in great need,
praise him, uphold him
now and forever.
Slow to fall into more sin.

Alleluia, Alleluia
To the Lord my praise I sing

Praise the Angels that surround him
Way up high in heaven above
Praise him for his tender mercies
Swift to bless, and slow to scorn

Alleluia, Alleluia
To the Lord my praise I sing

We have a gospel to proclaim

We have a gospel to proclaim
Good news for everyone,
Jesus Christ has risen
Ascended up to heaven.

Telling of his birth in Israel
Not born in hall or house,
But born to be a king
In a stable all so bare.

Tell of his death on the cross
Salvation for us all,
That we may live in heaven
As Jesus allowed us to.

Now we rejoice to name him king
Our cross he often bares,
Our sins are on his shoulders
Our troubles tell him so.

Spirit of God

Spirit of God, descend upon me
Take hold of my heart
Through all my pulses, move
Stoop down on my weaknesses
Mighty as you are
No sudden rendering
As my feet are of clay.

I ask for no dream
Nothing to hold me
Spirit of God, descend upon me
No angel visiting
I deserve not
Save first my soul
From this torn heart.

Spirit of God, descend upon me
Teach me to feel that you are real
And make me love you as I should
Spirit of God,
descend upon me.

I hear a voice calling

I hear a voice calling
Somewhere in the distance
A man's voice
So loud
So proud
Rejoicing his good news
I cannot yet see him
But he's drawing near
He sounds happy
So eager to please
His love is overflowing
For I know not why
I guess he's young
Not old and grey
But proud enough to stand tall
He's over 6'5"
But I'm so short
So stout and fat
Not like him
Who's proud and loving
And glad to be alive

The voice of God

The voice of God goes around the world
His glory speaks for itself
The great king heralds his triumphant return
To the Garden of Eden
He goes within
From Star to Star
Country to country
A light for every nation
Colour and creed
Anointed with the spirit
Three in one
I shall praise him
Glory to the king
No broken Angel shall ever sing
But an uplifting voice shall be heard
From kingdom to kingdom
Planet to planet
The blind shall see
The lame will walk
And prisoners will laugh at their freedom
For God is with everyone
In heart and in kind
So,
The voice of God goes around the world
His glory speaks for itself.

Low in the Grave

Low in the grave he lay
Our deepest, fondest king
To rise again with the living
To ascend among us
As our friend

We rolled the stone away
Away from his tomb
To find no sign
Of our lord
Except the clothes that lay
On stone that wrapped our king

Death cannot hold him in
For he rises among us
To be forever in our midst
To be in glory above all others
Forsaking our Lord and king

For we sing his praises
To our lord and king
Death cannot hold him
Our lord, saviour and king
The one
Jesus Christ

Oh praise the Lord

Oh praise the Lord
Praise the Lord
To him in the highest
Praise the Lord
Praise the Lord
For he rules the earth
Oh come and behold him
For the good he has done
And worship before him
As you sing your songs

Oh praise the Lord
Praise the Lord
How can we rejoice?
Praise the Lord
Praise the Lord
For he is our host
Oh come kneel before him
In worship and praise
To love and adore him
Now and forevermore

Praise the Lord
Praise the Lord
Let the people rejoice
Praise the Lord
Praise the Lord
To he who is blessed
We worship and love him
To live in his heart
And one day we shall meet him
In his holy home

You are God and we praise you

You are God and we praise you
Our eternal light at the end of the day
All of mankind worships you
Our loving lord Jesus Christ

You are God and we praise you
Our God, the King of glory
You enrich our lives
Take hold of our hearts
And the angels all adore you

You are God and we praise you
King of all the glory
You overcame the pain
Rose from the gladdened rags
Into the riches of heaven

Come then, Lord, help us decide
On the path of righteousness
Be us in heaven
In a blanket of light
Or down below
Walking the earth

The Glory of the King

The glory of the king was seen,
"Hallelujah to the King!"
For he reigns on high
Our most loving Lord,
Our Saviour always on high,
And people ran and waved and cheered
'Hallelujah to our King most high!'

The glory of the King was seen
Around the universe,
For he made the plants, the people
and the animals,
The air we breathe and live by
So praise the Lord,
O chosen One,
Praise him with great adulation
For he is always with us,
In our sleep, and at our play,
He knows our wrongs,
He knows our rights,
For he is human,
He is the King!

Father, hear our prayer.

Father, hear our prayer
In times of need and good,
When we are hurting,
When we are too proud,
Father, hear our prayer.

Father, hear our prayer,
In times of happiness and lowliness,
For when we sin
It is with terrible sorrow
And we come to you for good.

Not for ever in green pastures
Do we want to walk,
But to be at your side
From this day on
Now and for evermore.

Be our strength in times of weakness,
Be our salvation in times of anger,
Be always there at our side,
Father, hear our prayer.

Jesus, my truth, my way

Jesus, my truth, my way,
On his shoulders he does bear
My cross of sin,
My glad rejoicing,
To pronounce to all
He is King.

Let Jesus be my wisdom, my guide,
My Counsellor, my strength;
Oh, leave me not,
Stay at my side,
Now and for evermore.

Through the fire and water you do bring
Anointment to fill my cup;
When all sin is at last destroyed
Let me be there
At a new awakening,
At a brand new dawn.

Oh make us all like you
In strength and wisdom,
And at our birth
When perfected in grace,
Will we hold to you
In your everlasting arms.

I heard a voice

I heard a voice,
The voice of Jesus
Saying to me:
'Seek and you shall find.'
The voice of Jesus
So loud,
So Clear,
Promising me many things
If I try so hard.
I felt my head upon his breast,
Heard his gentle voice so quiet, so proud,
Telling me all my darkest sins
That I have ever encountered.
I find in Jesus my resting place,
My home, my garden,
Just like his;
Not a stone that tried to hold him,
But a garden, just like mine.
I heard a voice,
The voice of Jesus
Saying to me:
'Seek and you shall find.'

The Lord is King

The Lord is King!
I stand in the midst of his glory
To worship him
And to adore him
To behold him for evermore.

The floods have lifted up, O Jesus,
Now we walk beside you
But mightier than the sound of many waters
Is our beating hearts.

The Lord is King!
I stand before you
In unison with our beholden Lord.
Come let us sing:
'The Lord is King!'

Your heart is very pure
Wash and cleanse our own,
Uphold us in your never ending love
To take away our sin,
To love you for evermore.

In the Snow-filled universe

In the snow-filled universe
That Jesus Christ made true
Came the baby Jesus
Laid out on his bed,
For he shines around the world
Lighting up the skies
In the snow-filled universe
That Jesus Christ made true.

For he is my Saviour,
My Beholder, Lord and King;
For he gives us blessings
Of many, many things.
He shows infinite wisdom
Of every blessed thing
In the snow-filled universe
That Jesus Christ made true.

Our God in heaven adores us,
He lights up our world
To give to us, receive us
From the sinners' world;
For he knows our failures,
No doubt there are many
In the snow-filled universe
That Jesus Christ made true.

We have a gospel to proclaim

We have a gospel to proclaim,
Good news for everyone,
Jesus Christ has risen
Ascended up to heaven.

Telling of his birth in Israel,
Not born in hall or house,
But born to be a King
In a stable all so bare.

Tell of his death on the cross
Salvation for us all,
That we may live in heaven
As Jesus allowed us to.

Now we rejoice to name him King,
Our cross he often bears,
Our sins are on his shoulders
Our troubles tell him so.

God is always

God is always on your side;
He is there through good and bad,
In all your doubts
And all your sins;
He forgives you
In all you say,
Even when you stray from the path;
He picks you up and carries you
In all your troubles
And your ills;
He's with you
Every day.

Jesus is my Saviour

Jesus is my Saviour,
He touches me every day
To heal my wounds
And teach his ways
To bathe in his glory
To receive the cross
On which he died,
For he loved us all;
He came back to us
From the cross of death
To be resurrected,
With a glowing halo
Around his head.
Jesus is my Saviour,
He reaches out and touches,
His love engulfs me,
His heart is true,
His mother pure,
And father true.
For both Mary and Joseph received
Their son so holy,
Only to die
For us all.

God gave us a purpose

God gave us a purpose
To live on earth;
God gave us a purpose
To live on earth;
He took us and fed us,
Gave us clothes,
God gave us a purpose
To live on earth.

God gave us his Son
So to take away sin;
God gave us his Son
So to take away sin;
He holds us
And cares for us
In his arms;
God gave us a purpose
To live on earth.

Our Lord Savior;
Risen for us
Our Lord Savior
Risen for us;
He took us
And fed us
cared for us;
God gave us a purpose
To live on earth.

I love you, O Lord

I love you, O Lord,
For you are a tower of strength;
The cords of the grave
They do not hold me
for I'm with you
In your Kingdom Come.

I Love you, O Lord,
For you have saved me;
You brought me to a place of liberty
And rescued me
From Immortal sin.

chorus)
I love you, my Lord,
For you have saved me;
You have saved me!
You have saved me!
I love you, O Lord,
For you have saved me!
You have saved me"

Heaven

Up in heaven I see stars,
Stars and a fountain;
Peace and serenity cover this land,
The people smile,
And feel no pain.
Where once there was pain,
Agony and torment,
Now there's only peace.
I'd like to go to heaven
See my Maker and the others;
Sing in eternal bliss,
Play a harp,
Wear a long robe,
Fear no evil,
Because none is there.
Up in heaven I sense peace,
Serenity and a bed.

Trees

'You are a planting of righteousness.' says the Lord,
A planting that He might be glorified in this nation,
Flourishing like a palm tree, growing like a cedar of Lebanon.
You are planted in the house of the Lord.
You shall flourish in the courts of God.
You shall bear fruit in old age – much fruit, fresh & flourishing.
You are rooted and built up in Christ.
You are trees planted by the river of life, feeding from the
life-giving waters that flow from the temple,
trees that produce fruit each month – good fruit, lasting fruit;
And your leaves are for healing – healing the sick, healing the
    broken hearted.
You are strong trees that will give shade to saplings growing up
    under your branches.
You will bear much fruit – intercession, salvation, teaching,
    fathering and wisdom.
You are trees like the olive and fig that honour God and bless
man. Bring glory to God by your leaves and branches, different
fruit according to different seasons, because you are continually
watered by the river which is Christ, drawing your sap and your
virtue from Him.

I waited patiently

I waited patiently for the Lord
To open my heart
And let him in;
I surrendered to the cross
And kissed his holy feet.

And he has put a new song inside me,
A song of thanksgiving
And set my feet tapping;
My feet are now upon a new-found rock,
The rock of Jesus Christ.

Blessed is the man who makes everything holy,
Blessed is his name up high;
For he gave us his holy heart
And he surrendered to the cross.

I waited patiently for the Lord
To put a song in my heart
And set a firm foothold
In the waters that caress me.
I give thanksgiving to the Lord.

You are God and we praise you

You are god and we praise you,
Our eternal light at the end of the day;
All of mankind worships you
Our loving Lord Jesus Christ.

You are God and we praise you,
Our God, the King of glory;
You enrich our lives,
Take hold of our hearts,
And the angels all adore you.

You are God and we praise you,
King of all glory;
You overcame pain and death,
Rose from the gladdened rags
Into the riches of heaven.

Come then, Lord, help us decide
On the path of righteousness;
Be with us in heaven
In a blanket of light
Or down below
Walking the earth.

Jesus is my Saviour

Jesus is my Saviour
For he reigns on high
To take me in his arms
Protecting me
And all I do.
For he is the anointed one
Honest, down to earth and true;
For he shows us mercy
In everything we do.
He does not bear us grudges;
He takes away our sin
To free us from all tyranny
And to cleanse us in all things..
Jesus is my Saviour
For he reigns on high
Protecting me
In everything I do.

No other place

No other place but the Cross
Can give any hope to me;
A sinner am I, so unsure of myself.
No other word, but the word of Jesus,
No other water, but the water of Jesus,
No other cleansing, but the cleansing of Jesus,
No other blood, but his own.
No other place but heaven
Can heal this sore head;
For friends may come,
And friends may go.
No other place but the Cross
Can give any hope for me.

I waited patiently

I waited patiently for the Lord
To open my heart
And let himself in;
I surrendered to the cross
And kissed his holy feet.

And he has put a new song inside me
A song of thanksgiving
And set my feet tapping
My feet are now upon a new found rock
The rock of Jesus Christ.

Blessed is the man who makes everything holy,
Blessed is his name up high;
For he gave us his holy heart
And he surrendered to the cross.

I waited patiently for the Lord
To put a song in my heart
And set a firm foothold
Through the waters that o'erwhelm me.
I give thanksgiving to the Lord.

Lord of hosts and glory

Lord of hosts and glory
Glorified in name,
Holy to the highest
On the Earth be praised;
For it's you we honour
In your redeeming way,
Glory to the angels
Hosannah to the hosts.

For we obey and honour,
We seek peace and love,
Glory to the angels
Simplified in praise..
We bow down and honour
God's own son, Jesus,
For he's loved in me and you,
He is praised on high.

Lord of hosts and glory
Jesus in heaven above,
He walks the earth with you,
Carries you until the end.
We will praise and honour
We will sing the songs
Until we're with our Maker
Sitting way up high.

Dear uniting love

Blessed are those in dear uniting love
That will never depart;
Their bodies may be far removed
They are still in one's heart.

Joined in spirit
To the head
And in Jesus footsteps they tread
To glorify his praise.

We may always walk with him
To the very end
And know no more
The babbling brook of self-content,
But Jesus was crucified

We may always walk with him
In a united love;
Heaven and Earth ordain this
To the very end.

There is a Word in Jesus

There is a Word in Jesus
Who reigns on high
His soul never departed;
His love will overflow,
Constancy will be our guide;
His heart will rule over ours
Love will flow from in between
The arms that never let go.

There is a Word in Jesus
That love will conquer all;
Our place in heaven will be
Enfolded in his arms
In pure harmony,
Resting at his side
For eternity and evermore.

There is a Word in Jesus
Come, rest by my side,
Take the chains away of sorrow
Come, rest at my side,
A new life now reigns,
A new beginning with no end,
Where peace and harmony regain their place,
Living to the end.

Lord, you have been our Refuge

Lord, you have been our refuge
In times of uncertainty,
In times of anguish;
You have always been there
As a friend and protector
To see everyone on their way,
Through life and death.
We are consumed by your anger,
Our hearts are always with you,
Our hands are willing to serve,
You can cut life short
Or prolong it.
Who can know your transgressions
Except those who pray to you
Around the World, to heaven above?
Our days decline,
Our lives are numbered,
From eternity you came
Where we will go
To sit by your side
For evermore.

Oh, give thanks to the Lord

Oh, give thanks to the Lord
For he is good.
He is your salvation,
Your rising and your death.
The Lord is a tower of strength,
Joy and deliverance.
I shall not die, but live
In the home of the Lord above.
So, to the gate of the Lord I go,
The stone that the angel upturned
To reveal the Lord had risen
To heaven up above.

See the great High Priest

See the great High Priest
On his throne for evermore;
Whatever the Earth provide
He will always be in Heaven
And I will be at his side.
See the great High Priest
One body, and one vine
Outstretched hands with thorn marks in,
Blood dripping from his side,
Never a word in anger.
The people of Israel declare
Praise, the coming Lord,
For he is the King
Above all others.
See the great High Priest!

We have a gospel to proclaim

We have a gospel to proclaim
Good news for everyone,
Jesus Christ has risen
Ascended up to heaven.

Telling of his birth in Israel
Not born in hall or house,
But born to be a king
In a stable all so bare.

Tell of his death on the cross
Salvation for us all,
That we may live in heaven
As Jesus allowed us to.

Now we rejoice to name him king
Our cross he often bares,
Our sins are on his shoulders
Our troubles tell him so.

Preserve Me, O God

Preserve me, O God,
For in you I have taken refuge,
To anoint me,
To caress me,
To uplift me
In your arms.

Preserve me, O God,
Feed me with your love
For I have sinned
Above all odds,
Anoint me with your love.

Preserve me, O God,
I will bless the Lord,
Therefore my heart is glad,
My spirit rejoices
That I am at one with God.

God's Greatest Word

It was like a breath of fresh air,
God's greatest Word;
For he gave to us his only Son,
Jesus.
Born of Mary,
He died for our sins,
He gave us life,
Jesus.
Who loves everybody,
A light in the darkness,
A heavenly Being
Declaring
God's greatest Word.
Let the words of the Almighty
Overwhelm my soul,
My life,
My all.

Blessed is the Lord

Blessed is the Lord
For he reigns on high,
He reigns on high,
He reigns on high.
Blessed is the Lord,
He reigns on high,.
He reigns on high

He is my Saviour,
Praise be to the Lord,
Praise be to the Lord,
Praise be to the Lord .
He is my Saviour,
Praise be the Lord,
Praise be the Lord.

The Lord is my strength
And my salvation,
And my salvation,
And my salvation.
The Lord is my strength
And my salvation,
And my salvation.

Blessed is the Lord
For he reigns on high,
He reigns on high,
He reigns on high.
Blessed is the Lord,
He reigns on high,
He reigns on high.

From the Lord of the World

Comes a joyous heart
For he brings with him warmth, comfort
And good things
That only he can bring.
He delivers all of us from evil.
He will rest our weary bones.
He will be there in our bad times
And even in our sadness
When we are just run down.
In our happy days
He is there to guide us.
The Lord is our protector from the bad.
He washes away our sins
From the Lord of this World.
He comes in plenitude, with many offerings
That he showers all around us.
He loves a cheerful giver
Who helps mankind in many ways.
He releases us from the devil
And condemns the Satan curse.
The Lord of the World is Jesus
And I pledge my troth to him
For he will always protect me,
In the good times
And the bad.

Hear me, O shepherd of Israel

Hear me, O Shepherd of Israel,
You that lead your flock to pasture;
You that are enthroned upon high;
Before Man, I pray that
Your Kingdom come, for evermore.

Hear me, O Shepherd of Israel,
You have fed us with your love,
You endow us with your wisdom ,
You have cried tears over us
Through your undying love.

Hear me, O Shepherd of Israel,
Restore in us the faith of God,
Enrich our souls with your peace
Like the Doves that fly up high,
Gracious as your love.

You cleared the ground before us,
You enriched our souls,
You raised our hearts,
So that there is peace
And harmony
For evermore.

Graces (i) for Brian Barnard

Lord, thank you for this food,
The drink we sip
And the friends we have;
Thank you for our teachers,
Thank you for our church.
Amen.

Lord God, you touch our hearts
Thank you for Boys' Brigade,
Thank you for a safe journey,
Thank you for your Son
In his teachings to us
And to our friends.
Amen.

Jesus, you touch our hearts,
Protect our teachers and our many friends,
Protect our church,
In its every calling.
Protect our pastor
And his preachings.
Amen.

Thank you for our church
For the meal that we shall eat
And the drink that we will sip,
The teachings that will refresh us,
The games we play
And the tents that we build.
Thank you for your guiding Hand
Protecting us now and for evermore.
Amen.

Guide us on safe journeys
Wherever Boys' Brigade may lead
From our church,
If to a field
To play our games,
And build upon your teachings
Guide our hands in your skills,
Building new things
And listening to the old.

Graces (ii) for Brian Barnard

Lord, protect us for safe travel,
For the food that you provide
And the drink that we shall have.
Protect us from the night
And safe into the break of day.
Take us on safe journeys
Until we're safe at home.
Amen.

Lord, bless our church,
The young and old inside
And the sick and needy, too;
Our teachers listen to your Word
Passed on by you for us to hear.
We are keen to learn your Word
And note our teachers well.
Amen.

Lord, thank you for Jesus,
Your son in Heaven
Who watches over us,
Who watches our friends,
When with us, and when not,
Who guides us on to greater things,
In childhood, and as an adult.
We learn your word now
And for evermore.
Amen.

I look forward to when next time we meet
Going home on a safe journey,
End of another Boys' Brigade,
Back home to our folk and church
To recall our memories;
Trophies we have won, or lost,
Applauding those who win
And clapping those who lose;
Giving them a hearty whack on the back
They did well to serve you, Lord,
But next time theirs is the prize.
Amen.

I Know inside my Redeemer lives

I know inside my Redeemer lives,
My heart sings out his songs;
By his love and everlasting love
He shines inside my heart.

May the Word of God move inside
Into this cold and heartless heart;
Fill us up with love anew
And redeem us from Satan.

Lord, that I may learn from you
To walk your path of righteousness;
Come, Father, teach us how to pray
And live inside your heart.

Of my boasted, wisdom spoiled
Young and helpless as a child,
Bring with you the truth of righteousness
So that I may walk in your light.

Stand, Soldier of the Cross

Stand, Soldier of the cross
First-begotten from the dead
With your face to the rising sun
With your robes well bled
And your anger gone.
Rise, ascend to Heaven,
Soldier of the cross,
Drink the true and living water
Eat the tasteless bread,
Turn wine into water,
Feed the many thousands,
Soldier of the Cross.
Though the lowest of the Word
You will not be forgotten;
You will reign in true Majesty
So stand, Soldier of the Cross.

One more step

One more step I go with you
Around the World
Around the Sun.
I walk in the shadows of my former self,
But now I'm in the sun
Worshipping you, O Lord;
Praying your every word
Until one day I'll be with you,
To see your face
And to touch your hands
That were pierced with a nail
To cherish your every word.

One more step closer to you,
Every day's a hurdle
Of life's ups and downs
And no great comfort
except in the comfort of your word.
And one day great exaltation
To see you,
To touch you.
So, one step closer to God I take
My mind at rest
And worry no more.

Blessed are those....

Blessed are those who do no wrong,
Who commit no evil
And in heaven will rule.
For they are saved
By his true Word,
The blessing from God
No man can undo;
No one can remain
Unless it's with God.

Blessed are those who are weak
For they seek strength
And God's salvation.
They learn of peace,
Freedom and goodwill
To be an ambassador of the Lord,
To seek eternal youth.

Blessed are those who are strong
For they inherit the Earth.
They comfort the needy,
Bring hope to the dying,
They pray every day for me and you
So that we will go to Heaven,
To be at God's right side
Now and for evermore.

So, Blessed are those....

As my soul pants for the water

As my soul pants for the water,
You alone are king,
To rejoice in your glory,
To bathe in your land.
Sacrifice and offerings are all I have.
In the scroll of the Book
I read your words,
Gentle, unobtrusive words
To hear your voice
And to see your vision,
To know that you are there
For now and evermore;
To drink the water
That you provide,
To praise you every day,
To uphold your every way.
From the great congregation
I love you, Lord,
And all that you do
For you are my provider
Of everything that is new.

I will bless the Lord

I will bless the Lord
Whose hand was heavy upon the world,
For he is King
And he reigns above.
To see the World
As the Lord sees it -
Beauty is all around
In our day-to-day lives.
I will bless the Lord
And say a big 'Thank you'
To our coming King,
The Creator of everything,
Including me and you;
To pray to him in Heaven,
To rest at his side,
To have a big 'Well done'
From our chosen Lord.
I will bless the Lord
With outstretched hands
With a heart full of pride
To bathe in his glory
Now and for evermore.

Great is the Lord most high!

Great is the Lord most high!
The redeemer of kings,
The Lord up above.
Prayer is a simple form
That the Lord gives to us.
Prayer is the burden of a sigh
In Gentle whispers to our king,
Who hears our every word
In every language under the universe.
Father, behold our dying hearts
While angels wrap us in their robes,
Great is the Lord most high!

Prayer is a Christian's vital breath.
The path of prayer goes on
Around the World,
Around the sun.
Great is the Lord most high,
Upward glancing of our eyes
When no one around is near.
The motion of our trembling hearts.
Great is the lord most high!

I call to my God

I call to my God
And surely he will answer
In the day of our distress.
I think upon God
And what he has done for us,
To see the World
As he sees it;
Not the violence therein
But a peace and serenity.
Restore us again, Lord,
So that we can have peace
In our lifetime and for evermore.
Show us the light
Of your peace and Heaven.
I call to my God
And He will surely answer.

Oh, praise the Lord!

I will praise the Lord with my whole body,
In the company of Angels
In the highest of the high
And among the congregation
I will sing on high.

His love is angelic,
His Heart is to proclaim
That he is the Lord
Who reigns upon high.

His words are in hands of the Almighty
Who speaks to you and to me;
His love is everlasting,
His faithfulness goes on.
I will praise the Lord with my whole body.

He showed Israel his way,
He took them on a journey,
He speaks to the sinners
And lays down his commandments.

Glorious Lord, Oh praise the Lord
With all my heart,
And all my desire
In the highest of the high
From the lowest of the low!

Give thanks to the Lord

Give thanks to the Lord
For he rules on Earth.
His word is the Gospel
And Creation was born from his hand.
We are his servants,
We are his spiri.t
Give thanks to the Lord
For he reigns on high.

To the gate of the Lord,
To the heart of the World,
He has become my salvation;
From now until I die
His message is clear,
His spirit is true,
He won't forsake you.
He will always be at your side.

The day will come that I shall die;
My spirit will be in Heaven,
My heart will be in Christ.
Give thanks to the Lord
For he reigns on high;
The spirit is willing
And life will never cease.

When the Lord

When the Lord turned to the cross
He wept in pity and Joy,
For his son on Earth was dead,
But in Heaven he now reigned supreme ,
The champion of the Angels,
The creator of all things.
He bore you into the world
He gave you a heart to love and trust.

Behold how good the Lord now is.
He tends you like his sheep.
He holds you forever dear.
Children are a lifeline
From generation to generation.
They will tend the elderly, sick and infirm,
Hold you in great stead.

Unless the Lord builds you a house
Your labour is not worth it;
For you shall tend his home
While you live on Earth,
And go home to him when you die.
Happy is the man who always smiles,
Sad the man who cries,
When the Lord turned to the cross
He wept in pity and joy.

Come, my Children, to the Lord

Come, my Children, to the Lord.
Listen to me,
I will teach to you the value of life,
I will keep your tongue from Evil
And stop your lips from lies,
Turn your good deeds into love,
Turn your Evil thoughts into goodly array.
Your eyes will be the eyes of God
To seek out your Lord's face,
He is close to those who believe,
He is far from those who go astray .
Your ears shall listen to his words,
Your heart will be so pure
Love will overwhelm you
And keep you by his side.
So fear not the face of Jesus,
He is always with you
Each day to the next.

Jesus is my Light

Jesus is my light
And he is my strength
He can also mean Salvation
For such a sorrowful world.
I have never asked for much
But many have been greedy.
The Lord has never raised them
To live in Heaven, only hell,
Where down below it's dark and hot;
Up above it's peace on Earth.
To see fair play
In a cruel world,
To find the peace
Of heaven over hell,
Jesus will be with me.
When my time will surely come
Which way I'll go
I do not know;
Only God is my Salvation
In this mixed up world.

Jesus is declared in Heaven

Jesus is declared in Heaven
To rule those who are there,
To listen to their moans
And take away their grief.
Happiness will always rule above,
If you love the Lord
There is no sorrow
No pain, no grief,
Only to be happy
And live like Jesus Christ.
The Lord is pure
And he is kind
His eyes are always caring,
His heart is as wide as big,
Your life he holds in trust,
And he never stops caring.
For he loves you lots
He died for you on the cross,
The rising of his body,
The robes he left behind,
Are all a sign of his coming
When time on Earth is dead.

Sing to the Lord

Why not sing to the Lord
With a raised voice
And bring offerings
Of your love and kindness
To worship at his feet?
To hear his voice so smooth and silky?
Majesty and Glory are all his,
Declare the wonders of his reign;
Beauty and power are all his,
We are just plain mortals
That worship at his feet.
We bring a song in our hearts
And praise with our mouths.
In a way we fear him
Because he's awesome and good.
Our hearts will always love him
We sing to the Lord in peace;
The rivers they swell with pride,
The seas just collide,
As God's voice is heard.
We obey and go with love.